Colourful reef fish while snorkelling at Namena

First published 2023 by Wildiaries

Melbourne, Australia.

ISBN   978-0-6454535-5-3

© Simon Mustoe, 2023

Illustrations & photos © Simon Mustoe, 2023

Welcome

The northern division of Fiji is a great place to snorkel but it's really hard to find anything online about where to go and what to expect.

In the hope it might help you with your visit, we wrote this guide after a month exploring southern Vanua Levu and Taveuni in August 2023.

You will no doubt hear about cyclone Winston that had a devastating effect on the reefs in 2016. Recovery has been extraordinary and not everywhere was equally affected. There are places where the coral might even be more abundant with unusual wildlife now, than before. This is no reason not to visit. As you will see, there is still plenty of reef in good condition.

Despite a reputation for being diving's poor-cousin you will see more snorkelling than diving, and mostly in only a few tens-of-centimetres of water. We travelled with the late Neville Coleman's book *Fiji Islands: World of Water Wildlife Guide* which illustrates 512 species. We saw 224, of which 207 were while snorkelling. Many are prized sightings by divers but were common on the inshore shallow reefs, especially at night.

For native Fijians the ocean is their life and almost everyone knows something about the sea. Many people you meet will have swum, snorkelled or even dived, in nearby locations. The gateway to this region is the sleepy town of Savusavu. Away from the hustle of the major cities, it is a charming mix of visitors and locals, keen to help you with your stay.

Savusavu is a peaceful and well-serviced harbour where you can walk the full length of the high street in less than ten minutes. There are well-stocked supermarkets, a range of eateries and a pleasant harbourside park and marina. But it's essentially a South Pacific Island. Don't expect to find well-developed tourism. If you have limited time, plan your trip before you go.

Best wishes,

Simon Mustoe, author, ecologist and conservationist
Visit **simonmustoe.blog**

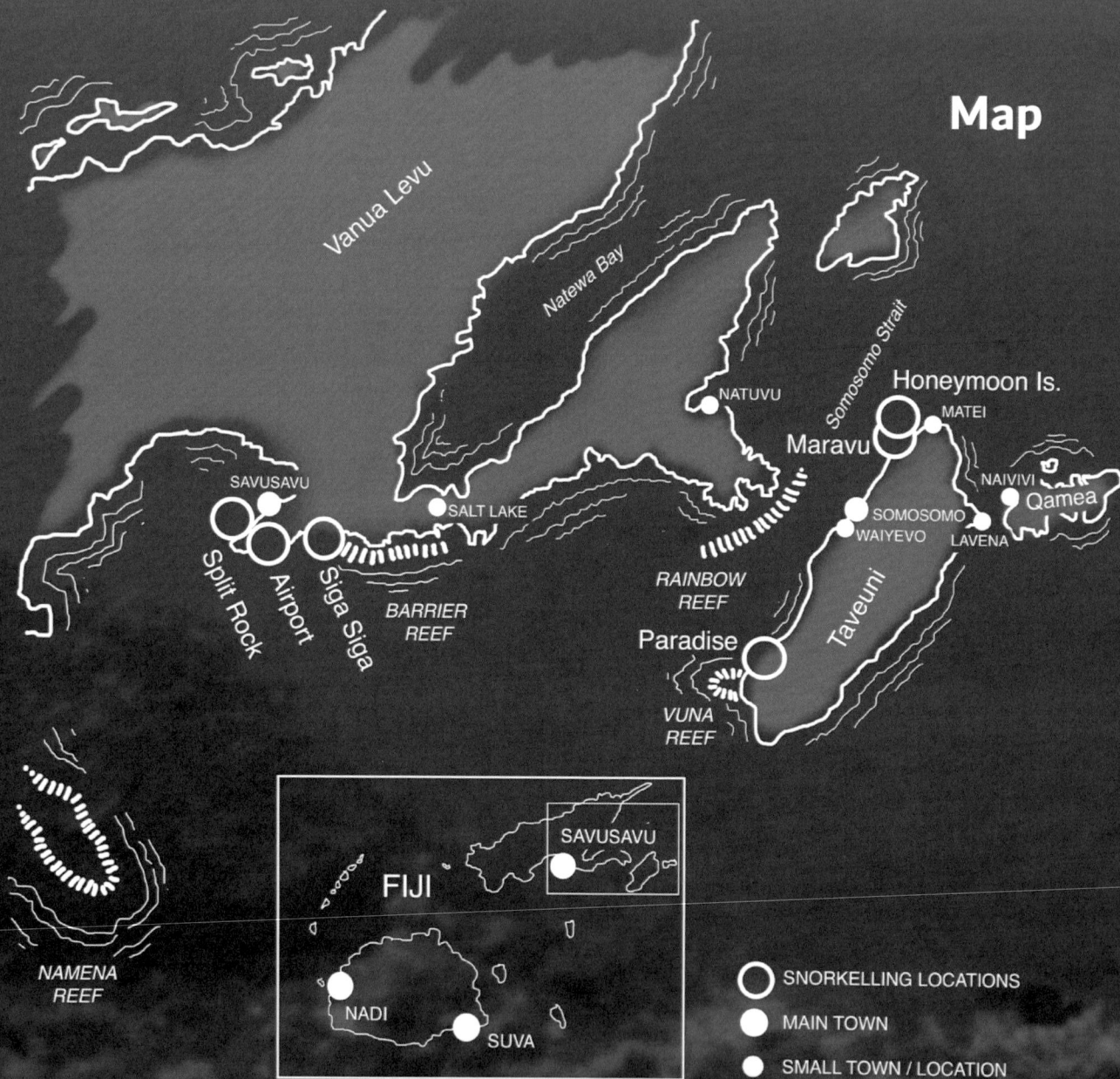

Map

Vanua Levu

Natewa Bay

Somosomo Strait

NATUVU

Honeymoon Is.

MATEI

Maravu

NAIVIVI

Qamea

SOMOSOMO

SAVUSAVU

SALT LAKE

WAIYEVO

LAVENA

Split Rock

Airport

Siga Siga

BARRIER REEF

RAINBOW REEF

Taveuni

Paradise

VUNA REEF

NAMENA REEF

FIJI

SAVUSAVU

NADI

SUVA

○ SNORKELLING LOCATIONS

● MAIN TOWN

• SMALL TOWN / LOCATION

Contents

Overview

Islands and reefs

Fiji's northern division mainly comprises the islands of Vanua Levu and Taveuni. Northern Vanua Levu is remote but Southern Vanua Levu, the west coast of Tavenui and Qamea, are easy places to plan a stay. Our travel took us from Savusavu all the way to Qamea.

There are four reef systems, plus Natewa Bay (see opposite page). These are serviced by different nearby operators. Most snorkelers will want to do a boat trip to Namena Reef and Rainbow Reef at least once. Natewa Bay is also well worth visiting.

Snorkelling sites and safety - IF IN DOUBT, DON'T GO OUT.

The sites detailed here are only a sample of possibilities recommended by locals. But not all are suitable for beginners. Many of the places you go in Fiji will be on the edge of open-ocean and include some reef edges and deep water. The next nearest land can be a quarter of a planet away! Paying attention to local conditions and weather (p37) is essential.

It's particularly important to be well-equipped and a strong swimmer (with fins) and not to wander anywhere unless you are absolutely confident about local currents and conditions.

In using this guide, you take full responsibility for your own safety and welfare. If in any doubt, do not venture beyond the shallows. Always swim with a buddy and let someone know where you are.

Organised tours

Organised tours (p30) are mostly designed to give visitors a peak at coral reef landscapes. Expect to snorkel over reef tops offshore in many cases.

Because boat trips generally don't go out in southeasterly winds above 20 kph, it's important to maintain flexibility in your schedule. Get in touch with the operators a couple of days before good weather is forecast and have your name added to lists to avoid disappointment.

But there are shore-based snorkelling sites on each island that are safe in most conditions and offer protection from the worst weather (within reason, no-one would advise travelling in cyclone season).

The best advice is to go with the expectation that for half of the time the weather may not be suitable to go out offshore, and the southern-facing coast may be too rough. In those cases, this guide gives you another option or two.

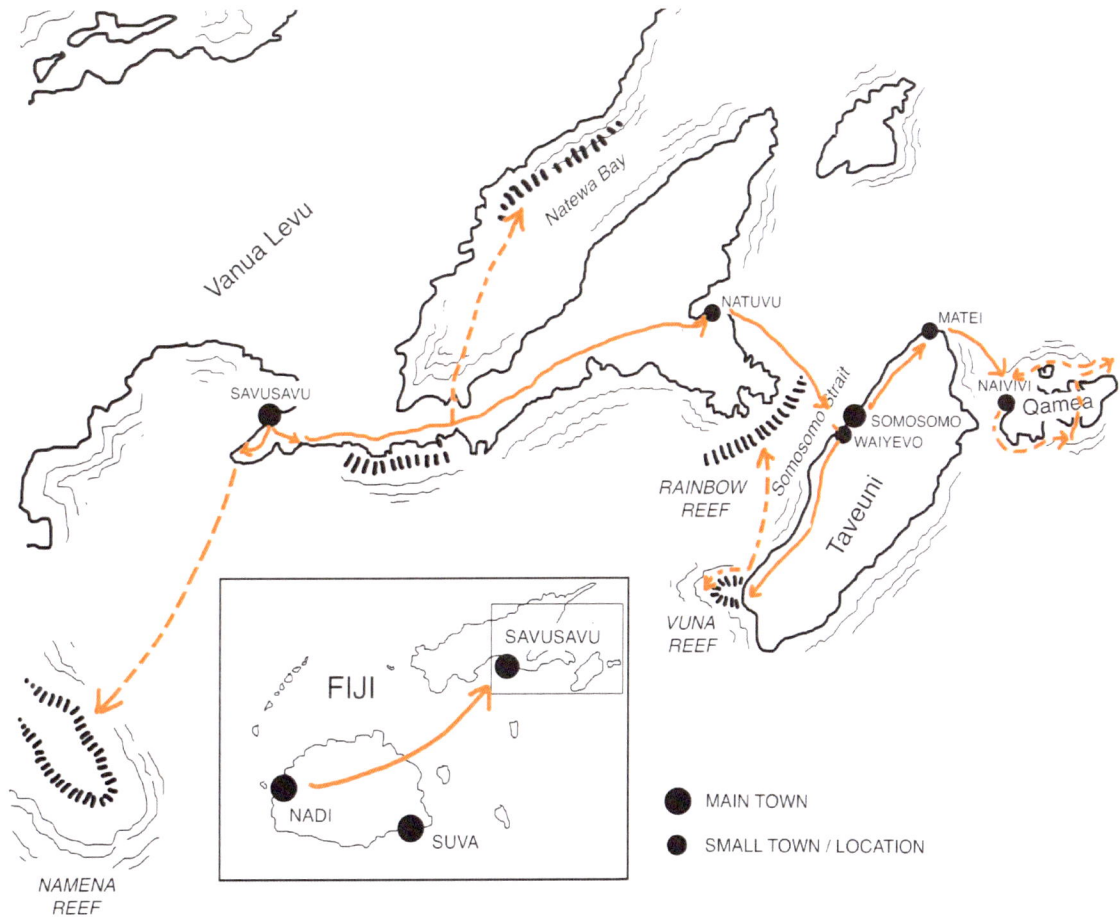

Vanua Levu

Natewa Bay

NATUVU

MATEI

SAVUSAVU

NAIVIVI

Qamea

SOMOSOMO
WAIYEVO

Somosomo Strait

RAINBOW
REEF

Taveuni

VUNA
REEF

SAVUSAVU

FIJI

NADI

SUVA

● MAIN TOWN

● SMALL TOWN / LOCATION

NAMENA
REEF

We combined shore snorkels with boat trips (dotted lines). Overall, we saw an incredible diversity of wildlife in a short space of time. Shore-based snorkelling isn't really possible on Qamea. We did a village homestay and took boat trips to the surrounding reef, which was also spectacular.

Equipment & Techniques

Staying warm and protected in the water

Do I need a neoprene (wet)suit?

Yes. Despite the warm water, you will find a wetsuit useful. It does get cold after an hour or so, especially when it's overcast, or at night. You can stack layers to achieve more warmth. A **normal wetsuit** will do. Good **thermal underlayers** can add the equivalent of an extra 1.5 - 2.0mm. For most people a 3mm wetsuit with 1-2mm of thermal layer provides flexibility for most conditions. A **hood** (5mm) is a really useful addition. Sixty per cent of your body heat is lost through the head, neck, ankles and wrists. You can double your swim time by wearing a hood.

A full-length wetsuit (recommended) offers additional warmth as well as protection from sunburn and stings. Stings are usually only minor but among the plankton can be small offshoots of jellyfish and hydroids which can cause irritation. Hydroids (that look like bunches of feathers) also adorn rocks. Sea slugs (nudibranchs) eat them to become poisonous. Brushing against hydroids can cause a few days of itching. Naturally you should always avoid touching coral but if you do, a wetsuit will also limit the risk of a coral cut and likely infection.

What is the water temperature?

Monthly water temperatures												
Month	JAN	FEB	MAR	APR	MAY	JUN	JUL	AUG	SEP	OCT	NOV	DEC
Temp °C	26-28	26-28	26-28	26-28	26-27	25-27	25-27	24-26	24-26	25-27	25-27	26-28

Reef shoes

Fiji's geology means many shore-based reefs are accessed by walking. Please tread lightly and carefully to avoid stepping on wildlife and never walk on the coral. There are sharp rocks, deadly cone shells and poisonous, camouflaged stonefish around, which is why it's best to walk on sand and look where you step. It's inevitable that you will need reef shoes though. We often snorkelled by stuffing the shoes down the top of our wetsuit after putting our fins on.

Mask, snorkel and fins

The only essential gear for snorkelling is a mask, snorkel and fins. You don't need anything fancy and as with most tools, it's how you use them that counts.

Snorkelling gear

ESSENTIALS

- Mask
- Snorkel
- Fins

THERMAL SUIT

- Wetsuit

UNDERLAYERS (Optional)

- Thermal top & leggings
- Hood
- Boots / socks / reef shoes

ACCESSORIES (Optional)

- Dive watch
- Torch
- Knife
- Camera
- Weight belt

How do I know if my mask fits?

Do the 'suction test' by placing it on your face and gently inhaling. The mask should 'stick' through suction alone. The strap is only there to stop it slipping off, not to pull it hard against your face. Also make sure the strap is positioned over the crown of your skull and not behind your ears. The straps split into two, so each half should sit comfortably above and below the crown.

How do I avoid mask fogging?

Fogging occurs when warm, moist air in your mask condenses on the cooler glass, after the lens comes into contact with cold water. There are three common reasons for mask fogging:

1. **You are breathing out through your nose.** Your breath is warm and damp. Breathe through your mouth (snorkel) only.

2. **You are putting your mask on your forehead.** Heat and sweat from your forehead gets inside. Wear your mask around your neck instead.

3. **Your mask has become greasy on the inside.** The solution is to apply some soap and water before rinsing. Do this before you leave home.

Chemicals promise to keep masks clear but none are necessary. It might sound gross but the tried-and-tested method is to spit inside your mask and rub it around with a finger before rinsing. As long as you've addressed #1-2 above, you should have no fogging problems.

New masks can also come with an invisible coating on the inside lens. This might need to be cleaned off by scrubbing lightly with toothpaste and rinsing a few times.

How do I avoid mask leaking?

Assuming you've done the 'suction test', your mask definitely fits. If your mask leaks in the water, there are usually two common reasons:

1. **You have something caught under the rubber seal.** Even a small amount of facial hair can cause leaking. Run your fingers around the seal after putting your mask on and check to make sure your hood or hair isn't trapped in the seal. If you have a beard or moustache, you might need to use Vaseline to create a seal.

2. **Your mask has been put on too tight.** The rubber seals around your mask are supposed to mould to your face. But if you over-tighten the straps, it causes the rim to buckle. The solution is to loosen the straps.

Your mask strap should split over the crown of your head and only be just tight enough to stop it slipping off.

Clearing your mask of water

Hold your head upright and secure your mask against your forehead. Then gently lift the bottom of your mask away from your upper lip while blowing out through your nose. This air will fill the top of the mask and push water out of the bottom. Re-secure the mask and carry on swimming.

How do I choose a snorkel?

This simple technology has been around for decades– it's only a pipe to breathe through after all. Make sure it is on the left side and the bend at the top faces backwards. Don't bite too heavily on the mouthpiece and get used to clearing it by blowing out hard if any water gets in (which will happen if you duck dive).

What type of fins do I need?

If you plan to use fins that have back-strap then you may need boots or socks. But this is mainly for comfort and to avoid blisters If not, a pair of slip-on fins are just as good. Average length or short fins are both fine for beginners.

How much weight should I use?

There is no one-weight-fits-all rule but if you over-weight yourself it can be life-threatening. It's usually unnecessary if you're wearing a 3mm wetsuit and don't intend to duck-dive.

Weights add drag and if you're unfit, you can easily get exhausted. **If in doubt, do not wear any weight.**

People will often use 1kg of weight per 1mm of wetsuit thickness. But you also sink faster as you get deeper because the air volume in your lungs and bubbles in your wetsuit decrease under water pressure.

A weight belt is a quick-release system onto which you thread weights that usually come in 1kg units. It's good to have weights distributed symmetrically on your sides or back with the buckle **at the front and on the right,** so in an emergency, you can quickly release and 'drop' the weights with a flick of your right hand.

You should be able to lie horizontally in the water wearing weights without sinking, or float vertically with a moderate lungful of air, while keeping your eyes and nose above water. You should only sink if you exhale. If you are struggling to stay afloat or your legs are sinking, you are over-weighted.

Before you consider swimming any distance with weights, try them in shallow water and get comfortable.

Preparation, swimming and duck-diving

Kitting up

Sit in waist-deep water wearing all your thermal gear (boots, hood, gloves and wetsuit) and weights if you use them. It's easiest to put your fins on once you're in the water. If you try to do this sitting down with legs in front of you though, you'll roll backwards. Instead, try kneeling and fold one leg at a time underneath. Prepare your mask by spitting into it and rinsing in seawater. If you have long hair, rinse this backwards away from your forehead so it doesn't get caught in your mask seal. Place the mask on your face and do the 'suction test', then pull the strap back over the crown of you head. If you're wearing a hood, run a finger around the front to make sure it's not underneath your mask's seal. Do a quick test in the water and you're ready to go!

How to swim while snorkelling

Don't use your arms or hands. Fish detect vibrations in the water. So, each time you splash or push your hands around in front of you, it disturbs them. It takes time to learn but with practice you will be able to manoeuvre using gravity currents, with minimal leg-propulsion. By saving energy you'll be more relaxed and have a longer and more enjoyable swim where you can focus on seeing wildlife.

1. Fold your arms across your chest, let them trail to your sides, or hold your hands together just in front of you – this will make you more streamlined.
2. Frog-kick for propulsion (like a breast-stroke kick) – this tends to keep your fins below water, which means you don't splash. It uses less energy and doesn't scare fish away. Keep your legs bent and fins lifted to avoid hitting coral.

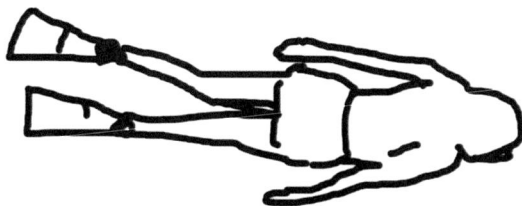

Do I need to hold my breath to snorkel?

No. Snorkelling can be done by swimming at the surface and breathing through your snorkel. As you gain confidence you may like to try duck-diving. But any activity that involves submerging yourself underwater of course comes with risk of drowning.

Breath-holding for long periods is a skill that freedivers have and can be dangerous. According to Divers Alert Network, mortality of untrained freedivers is 1 in 500, compared to 1 in 50,000 for competitive (trained) freedivers. Freediving changes your metabolism and training is used to help manage that risk.

Here I will go through a process of duck diving to depths or *no more than 3m* with breath hold of no more than about thirty seconds. Also, remember to equalise.*

Snorkelers who duck-dive to 2-3m and do thirty seconds underwater are not likely to breach metabolic thresholds that require skills training. In fact, duck diving is great fun and anyone can try it. But it is itself a skill and can be exhausting. So here are some hints and tips to help you learn.

How to duck dive

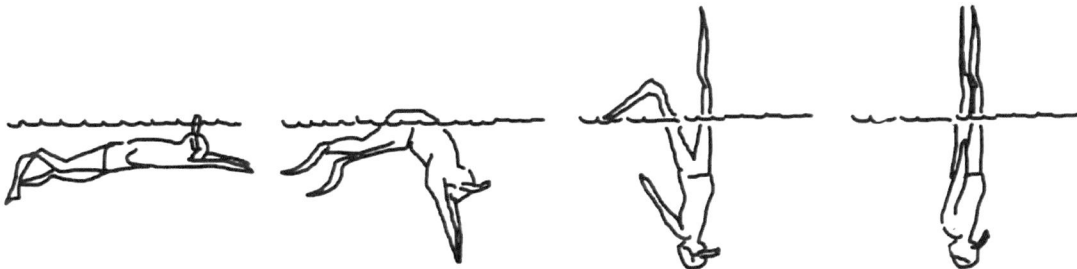

- Kick forward and put your arms out.

- Drop your arms.
- Let the shape of your body push your head down.

- Push one leg high in the air.
- Look behind you, as though doing a somersault.
- Begin lowering your arms to your side.

- Lift the other leg.
- Look down and place your hands by your side.
- Let your momentum take you deeper without kicking.

*To avoid ear damage, 'equalise' by pinching your nose and blowing out to 'pop' your ears. Do this before you dive, as you dive, and as often as possible as you descend. Pressure changes fastest near the surface so this is when you can hurt your ears.

8

How do I learn to duck dive?

Duck diving is something you need to learn. If you do it properly, you should be able to descend with little or no effort at all.

1. Close your eyes and meditate. DO NOT TAKE DEEP BREATHS as you risk hyperventilating. Breath normally from your diaphragm and **concentrate on reaching a relaxed state**.
2. Put your arms out straight with hands together to form an arrow and start to kick forward.
3. Lower your arms and 'arc' your body and keep kicking so your head goes down.
4. Double over as though you doing a 'head stand' (it may feel like a somersault).
5. Undulate your body so you sink vertically with little or no effort at all.
6. DO NOT USE YOUR ARMS TO GET DOWN (it uses too much energy – you should never have to use your arms for propulsion when snorkelling).
7. EQUALISE all the way down, to avoid hurting your ears.

Carry a dive knife for safety

If you are duck diving, especially around piers, you could get tangled in fishing line. A knife should be attached to your ankle on the right-hand-side. Make sure you know how to get hold of it quickly.

How long can I hold my breath?

See how long you can comfortably hold your breath sitting quietly on land. When you duck dive, you will manage about half that duration. Add 1 second for each metre of descent and ascent. For example, for a 3m duck dive:

Static breath-hold (in air)	1	min
Breath-hold underwater	30	sec
Descent time	3	sec
Ascent time	3	sec
Total time underwater	24	sec

When you start to feel you need to breathe, you might find it enough to raise your heart rate, using more air. If you know you can comfortably do 30 seconds, try counting. Or if you have a camera, run a video for 30 seconds.

Remember, each time you dive your oxygen gets more depleted and you have to recover longer at the surface. To help ensure you stay within your limits, REMAIN AT THE SURFACE BREATHING GENTLY for *twice the length of time* you were underwater.

Needless to say, swim with someone else. Although it's unlikely you'll pass out from a duck dive, there are many reasons why it can happen. Swimming with a buddy is extremely important anyway, as there are many reasons why ocean swimming can be dangerous.

Top places to go snorkelling

Here are seven places we snorkelled regularly. There are a range of sites to suit different skills and ability but remember, weather and tides are a key consideration for any ocean swimming. So, we've also recommended some sites on each island that are usually sheltered, with calm water and gentle currents.

Split Rock (Vanua Levu) *Grade = Easy*

Split Rock is the most famous snorkelling location on Vanua Levu. However, most people only find the car park and surrounding rocks, missing the site itself, which is situated 180m from the beach entry point. If you swim towards the two buoys, these are attached to a bommie about 50m on the shoreward side. You can't quite see Split Rock from there but if you swim away from the coast it will become visible almost immediately.

If you happen to be there around high tide there are often tourist boats visiting from nearby resorts. They feed the fish, so when you get close, you'll likely be swarmed by harmless Scissortail Sergeants.

Getting there

Split Rock is about 10 minutes by car from Savusavu and costs about FJ$10 by taxi. We usually arranged for our driver to pick us up two hours later.

Entry and where to go

Enter the sea where there is the sign and steps to walk down.

① A series of bommies to the north are increasingly diverse. Check the rock walls for moray eels, blennies and crabs.

② Look over the deeper open ocean parts. We saw the critically endangered guitarfish (a type of ray).

Conditions

Best snorkelled on a high tide when the top of Split Rock is accessible. Ideal in most conditions though near-shore visibility can reduce after a few days of heavy winds.

A slight surge is possible when strong winds are from the south, which can make it hard to pick your way along the edge of the shallow reefs and rock walls. Otherwise, currents are generally mild.

Some animals to look out for

Leopard Blenny, Scissortail Sergeants (many), Scorpionfish (on the reef), Stonefish (around the shallows), Fiji Anemonefish, Spot-fin Lionfish, Mirror Basslet, Dwarf Hawkfish.

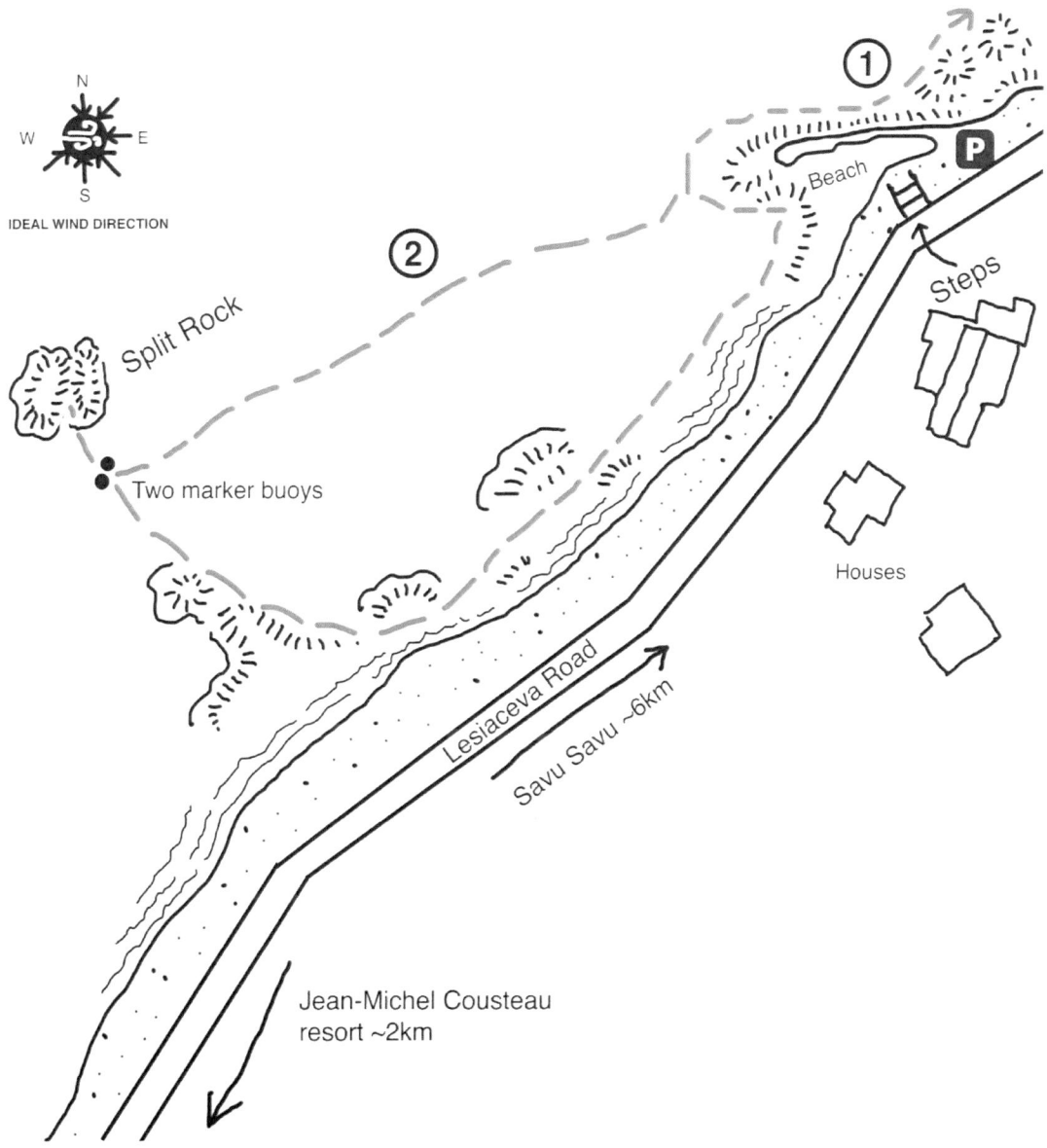

Images. Clockwise from top-left. The top of Split Rock; a Spot-fin Lionfish; Leopard Blenny; Sailors Eyeball (a massive single-celled algae).

Images. Clockwise from top-left. Small-scale Scorpionfish; the 'split' at Split Rock with Mirror Basslets; a Varicose Phyllidia sea slug; Dwarf Hawkfish.

Airport (Vanua Levu) *Grade = Moderate to Hard*

Getting there

About 5km drive south of Savusavu.

Entry point

There are resorts along the main beach which can make access a bit difficult.

If you start at the beach at the end of the air strip, walk east to the rocks standing on the reef flat.

Head out and look for a gap in the reef. It's about a 300m walk, so you will need reef shoes and you will have to carry everything with you. Arrange a pickup if you need, and allow at least two hours.

① Explore the extensive reef edge and the deep drop-offs between many bommies.

Conditions

⚠ Only snorkel this site in light northerly winds on a rising tide with minimal swell. ALWAYS TELL SOMEONE WHERE YOU ARE GOING. Best done after a day or two of good conditions.

Some animals to look out for

Hawksbill and Green Turtles, White-tipped Reef Shark, Black-tipped Reef Shark, Napoleon Wrasse.

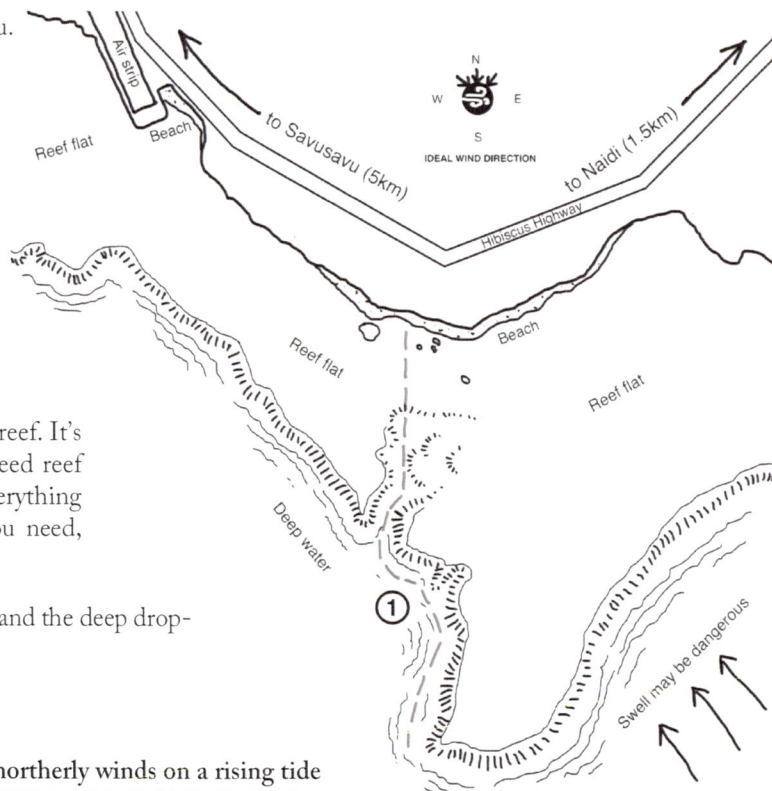

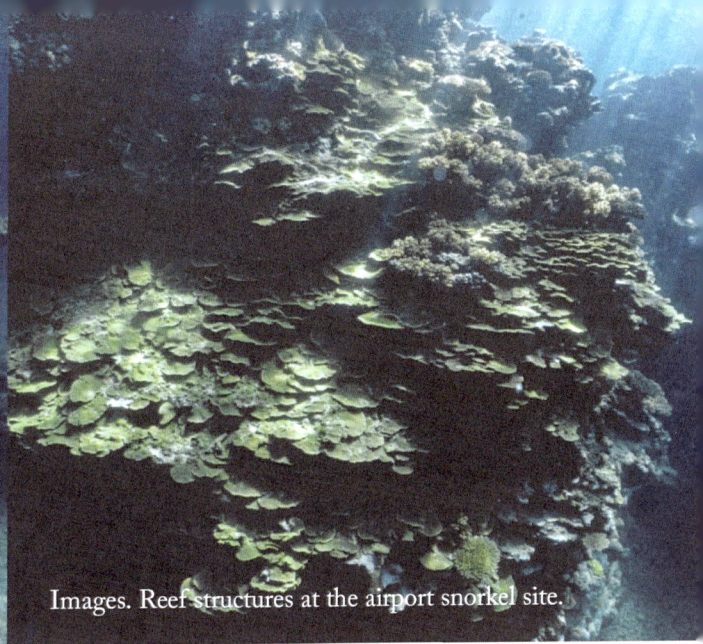

Images. Reef structures at the airport snorkel site.

A note on finding octopus

Octopus are common in Fiji and you can hardly fail to find one if you spend some time snorkelling. At SigaSiga Inner Lagoon, for example, they are abundant but are shy and live in tiny caves in the coral reef. When you find a pile of broken shells and pieces of crab below a piece of coral, it's usually an octopus that put them there. They are messy eaters. In the image (below right) the octopus is holding a shell up to the entrance next to its dinner left-overs.

If you find an octopus out in the open, stay back and watch. They are quite curious and given some time, will often come out and take a closer look at you.

SigaSiga Inner Lagoon (Vanua Levu) *Grade = Easy*

Getting there

Situated 11km east of Savusavu and about FJ$15 by taxi. Drive through Naidi village and continue another 4km.

Entry & where to go

If you are staying at SigaSiga Sands, walk west for 470m along the beach. Otherwise, there is an access track on the Hibiscus Highway.

① Lots of diversity. Including reef pipefish, many octopus (look for the remains of large crabs piled up next to holes). Many reef fish, batfish etc.

② Banded Snake-eel are quite common, which look a bit like a sea snake.

③ The reef flat comes alive at low tide. Green Mantis Shrimp, Peppered Moray and Brittlestars are abundant in the very shallow pools.

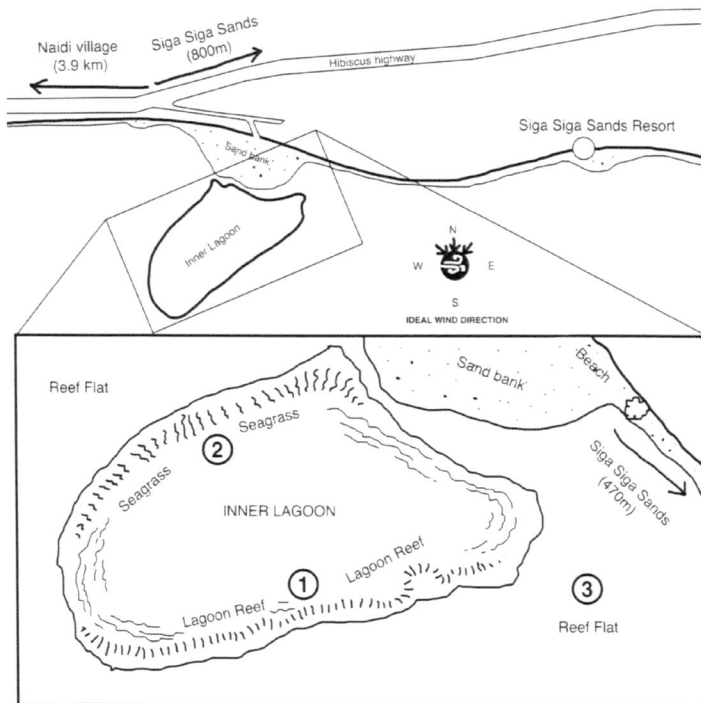

Conditions

This location can be snorkelled in almost any conditions at low tide. It's also good at high tide but if the wind is blowing strong from the southeast, a wind-driven current will push you west and it can get choppy at the surface. Even though it can appear murky most of the time, there is still a lot to see. This is are very productive nearshore site. It's also a wonderful place to night-snorkel, if you have an underwater torch.

Some animals to look out for

Banded Snake-Eel, Day Octopus, Picasso Leatherjacket, Peppered Moray, Green Mantis Shrimp, Ringed sapsucking slug, juvenile sweetlips and batfish, Box Crab, Neon Damsels.

Images. Top to bottom. Stars and Stripes Pufferfish; Ringed Sap-sucking Slug; Banded Snake-eel; Tiger Cowry; Fiji Anemonefish; Brittlestar; Blue Sea Star Shrimp; Peppered Moray; Picasso Leatherjacket; Green Mantis Shrimp; Gymnodoris Sea Slug.

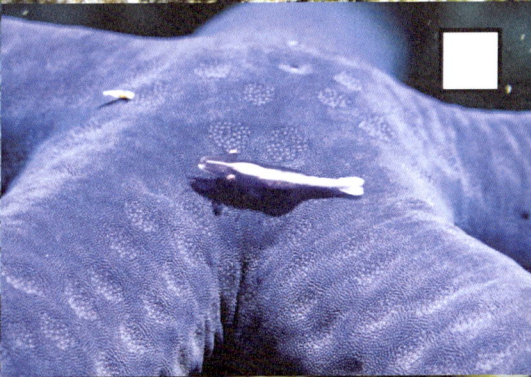

SigaSiga Outer Lagoon (Vanua Levu) *Grade = Hard*

This is an extraordinary snorkelling location. You could see almost anything here that you would see on the open ocean reef breaks. The snorkel described here is from the eastern end, where it is mostly protected from swell by the outer reef. Our best advice is to stay a few days and take your time. This way you can get the feel for conditions and your own abilities. This is best snorkelled in a northerly wind after a day or two of good conditions when swell is minimal. At high tide you will see ocean waves breaking on the inside edge of the reef. This abates at low tide but there are still some moderate to strong currents coming off the reef top.

Entry & where to go

Access is via the beach in front of SigaSiga Sands. If you are not staying, you may need to walk east (see 'Getting there' for the Inner Lagoon snorkel). The walk out is 650m across the reef so you will need reef shoes. Walk directly out to sea, aiming for the right-hand end of the line of exposed rocks (A). At low tide you will find a robust current running west on the inside edge of the reef (B) caused by seawater draining off the reef flat. You can cross this by moving between bommies but it's shallow. You will need to find a channel between them to get through into the deeper water (C). Once there, swim east against the current (staying close into the edge where it's easiest) until you reach calm water ①. Then drift-snorkel along the northern edge, stopping before the open-ocean opening ②. Then cross via the bommies to the north by swimming directly towards the nearest reef edge on the opposite side (this is steep and vertical, dropping to 30-40m or more) ③ before circling back. Exit in the little lagoon (D) where currents are minimal and it's very shallow.

Some animals to look out for

Goliath & Titan Triggerfish. Napoleon Wrasse. White-tipped, Grey Reef and Black-tipped Reef Shark, numerous nudibranchs, Hawksbill and Green Turtles.

① Goliath and Titan Triggerfish gather. Napoleon Wrasse present. White-tipped, Grey Reef and Black-tipped Reef Shark also occur.

② A channel forms between the inner reef and a 30m high bommie. To the west is open ocean. Spend time searching around this bommie for sharks and turtles.

③ Green turtle nursery. The turtles are shy and may swim away as you approach, so stay alert.

④ Search along the edge for colourful nudibranchs.

There are even whip-corals and patches of cabbage coral; (whip-coral shrimp and gobies do occur near the surface).

For additional guidance, See the aerial photo, next page, bottom left.

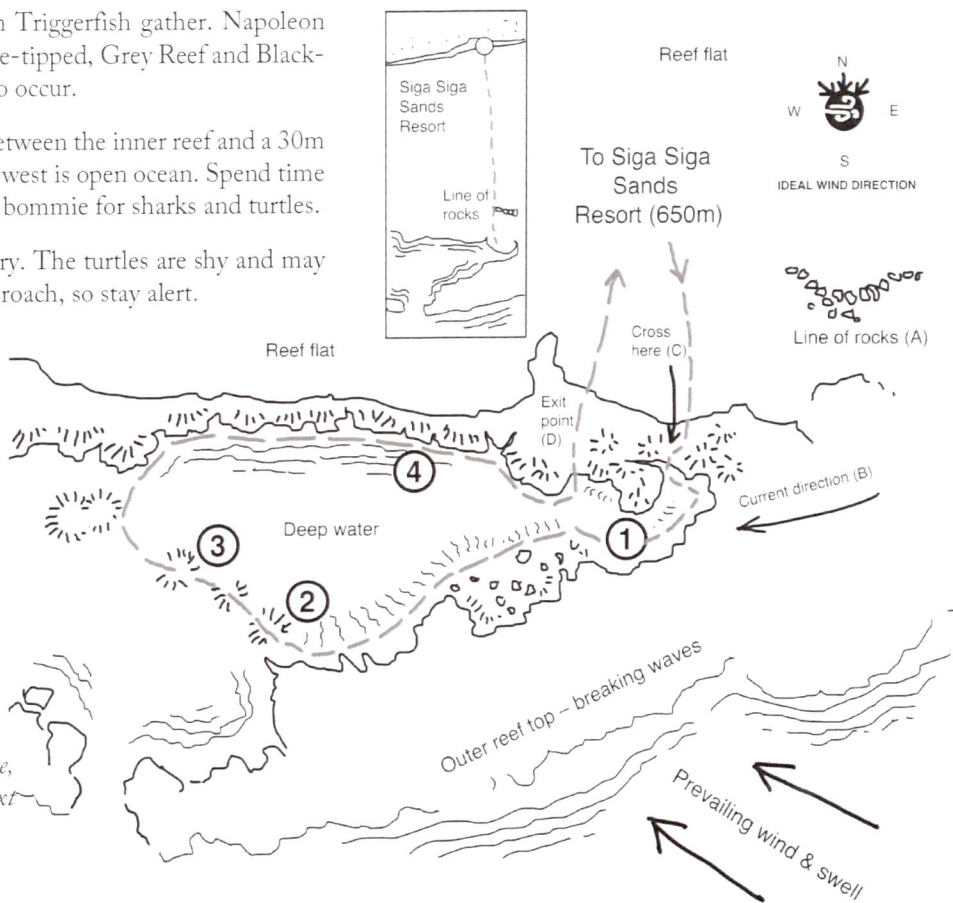

Siga Siga Sands Resort

Line of rocks

Reef flat

To Siga Siga Sands Resort (650m)

N
W E
S
IDEAL WIND DIRECTION

Line of rocks (A)

Cross here (C)

Reef flat

Exit point (D)

Current direction (B)

④

Deep water

③

②

①

Outer reef top – breaking waves

Prevailing wind & swell

Conditions

⚠️ Do not start this snorkel after low tide. Preferably begin walking out about one hour before. Note, low tide is about 1 hour before times shown for Savusavu.

⚠️ Only snorkel this site at absolute low tide with minimal swell. There can also be strong wind-driven surface currents which makes it treacherous outside of low tide.

⚠️ Do not attempt this unless you are comfortable with deep water swimming and are fit enough to snorkel for 1.5-2h without a break. ALWAYS TELL SOMEONE WHERE YOU ARE GOING.

Top: inner lagoon and outerlagoon; bottom-left: outer lagoon; bottom-right: inner lagoon.
Aerial photos of SigaSiga © Benjamin Hennig, Geoviews.net

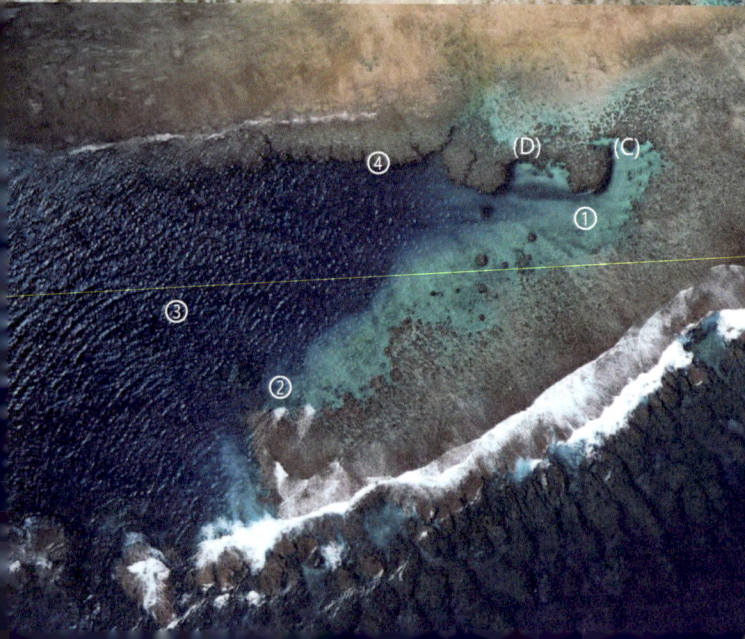

Images. Clockwise from top-left: Bommie in the outer lagoon; Flabellina sea slug; Blue-spotted Trevally; Green Turtle; White-tipped Reef Shark.

Honeymoon Island (Taveuni) *Grade = Moderate*

Getting there

Reached by kayak hired from Taveuni Ocean Sports (4km). Coconut Grove (2km) also has kayaks. They are usually happy to organise this with lunch if the accommodation isn't full (or you can stay there). It may also be possible to ask someone to organise a boat to take you.

Entry & where to go

You cannot start kayaking there until about 2h hour after low tide, or there is not enough water to cross the reefs.

① Tie your kayak securely on the beach to the north. Swim around the west and south. Rockmover Wrasse live in rubble over sand and seagrass just near the shore. Look out for Octopus too.

② Tie up on the beach on the SE side. Swim around the entire island. Explore the soft coral gardens, look for colourful sea slugs, reef sharks etc.

Conditions

If the wind is from the southeast, the sites are exposed and it is a difficult kayak. Allow at least one hour each way.

Honeymoon Island

Shallow reef

Coconut Grove

Matei

Air strip

Taveuni Ocean Sports

to Somsosomo (16km)

N
W   E
S
IDEAL WIND DIRECTION

Some animals to look out for

Black-tipped Reef Shark, Hawskbill Turtle, Rockmover Wrasse, Jewelled Blenny, Leather Soft Coral, Loch's Chromodoris Sea Slug, Day Octopus, Banded Sea Krait.

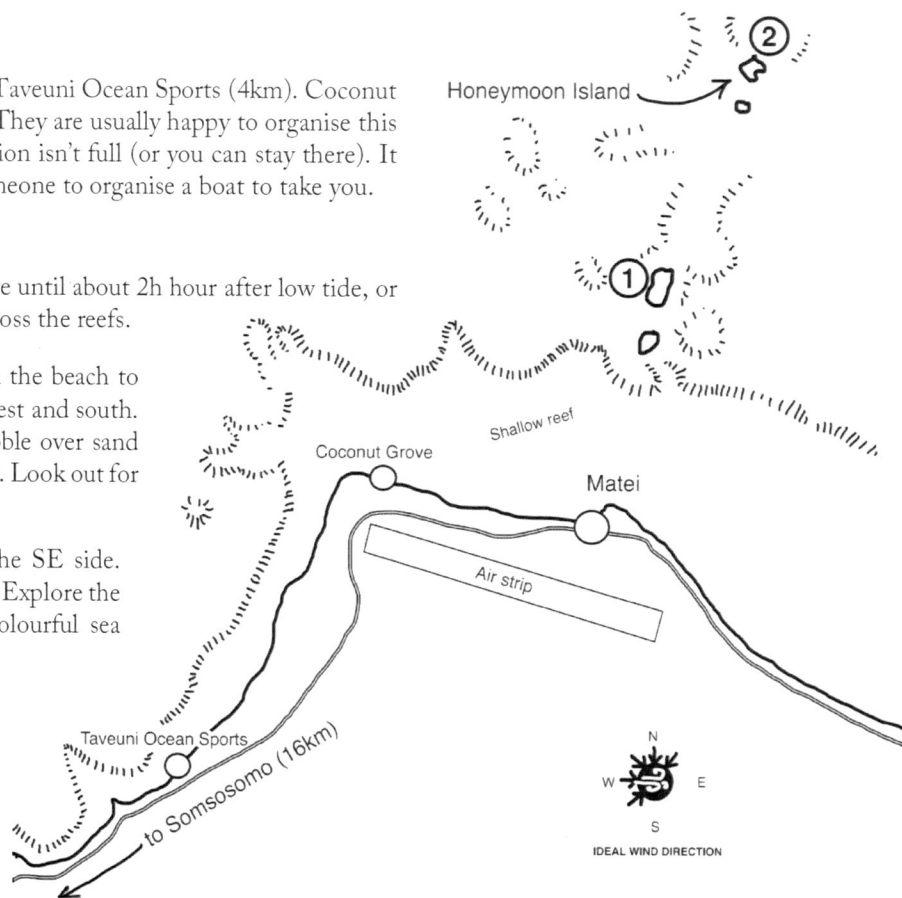

Images. Clockwise from top-left.
Hard and soft corals; view from
Coconut Grove to the islands;
Rockmover Wrasse; Purple
Staghorn Coral; Jewelled Blenny;
Minor Giant Clam.

Maravu (Taveuni) *Grade = Easy*

Getting there

Located at the N end of Taveuni, 2km south of Matei. There are lots of places to stay within walking distance.

Entry point

There is a café and watersports centre with a nice beach. You can leave clothing safely in front. Entry is best from the boat ramp (beware, this is slippery). At low tide, head slightly west and find the channel to head out. At higher tide you can swim into the adjoining bay between the promontory and offshore rocks.

① These coral rubble and seagrass areas are jam-packed with exciting animals. This is perfect place to night / sunset snorkel, and you only need 50 centimetres of water to see a wealth of wildlife. There are abundant anemonefish and hermit crabs. Look out for the Harlequin Leatherjacket.

② The inner reef is quite diverse but you need more water. This and the outer reef ③ are best snorkelled about 2 hours after low tide.

Conditions

This site can be snorkelled safely in pretty much any conditions. It's sheltered from the SE trade winds and northerlies tend to be light. Be aware of boat traffic from the water sports centre.

Some animals to look out for

Reef Pipefish, Banded Sea Krait, Harlequin Leatherjacket, Coral Hermit Crabs, Cake Urchin, Blue-spotted Hermit Crab.

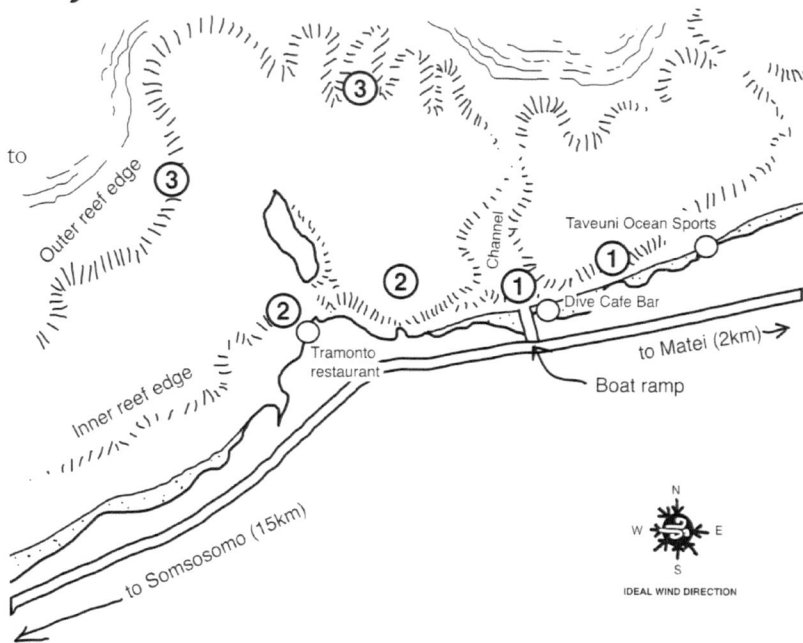

Images. Clockwise from top-left. Coral reef; Crown-of-Thorns Seastar; Blue-spotted Hermit Crab; Reeftop Pipefish; Banded Sea Krait; Geography Cone.

Paradise (Taveuni) *Grade = Easy*

Getting there

It takes about 1h by car from Somosomo, or about 1.5h from Matei. Half of this is on unsealed roads. If the roads have been wet a 4WD will be necessary. Expect to pay FJ$100 or more each way. If you are not staying on site but planning to have lunch, it's essential that you call the day before, as meals are finalised in the morning.

Entry point

Enter from the steps to the right of the pool, where the dive boats are moored.

① When swell permits, the rocky wall is a haven for so much diversity. Shrimp, pipefish, frogfish, octopus and Giant Morays have been seen.

② For beginners or young children, this area is full of shallow bommies covered with reef fish.

③ Adventure out to the drop off and there is a good chance of seeing White-tipped Reef Shark, different species of rock cod and lots more.

Conditions

Paradise Taveuni's house reef is second to none. There is nowhere else where you can swim right off the shore and be among intact and diverse coral reef. The conditions are almost always favourable but a swell can make it uncomfortable to swim against the rocks, although this is a great place to see a diversity of wildlife.

Some animals to look out for

There are hundreds of possible species. Reception has books to look things up. Common Lionfish and Giant Morays are quite abundant. Ocellated Dragonets live along the shore. Spend a few days building up a collection of sightings and you won't be disappointed. Or organise a guided snorkel with the resort.

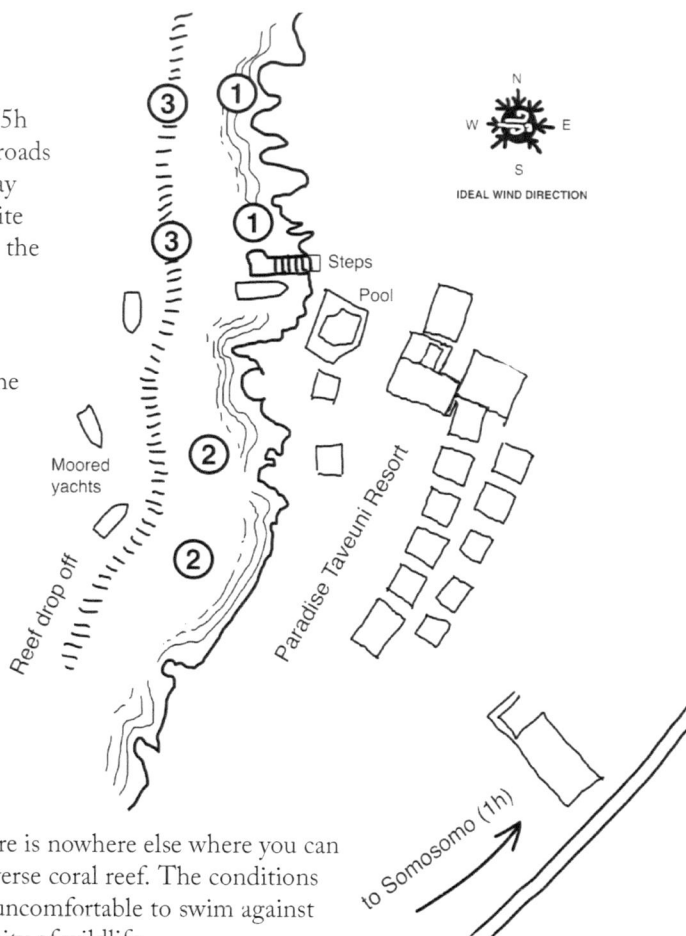

Images. Clockwise from top-left. Paradise Taveuni House Reef; Halloween Hermit Crab; Day Octopus; Ringeye Hawkfish; Ocellated Dragonet; Giant Moray; Common Lionfish.

Other day trips

There are a number of operators offering snorkel day trips. It's really worth doing some but you need to be aware of conditions.

Boat trips

These are mostly sightseeing trips to observe the fish spectacle. They tend to visit the most spectacular reefs but can be relatively deep and surrounded by open-ocean.

A visit would not be complete without at least seeing the Rainbow Reefs & Namena. These are colourful soft-coral systems covered with thousands of bright orange and purple fish (basslets).

Most operators also run dedicated near-shore trips. Your guides will be able to tell you which sites are coming up, based on forecasts.

Be aware that conditions often need to be less than about 10 knots (20 kph) to consider taking boat trips as otherwise, the Pacific swell can be atrocious. Namena Reef is the most exposed location.

If you're on Vanua Levu, Natewa Bay tends to be a little more sheltered but snorkelling spots are limited, so make sure you plan ahead.

The Rainbow Reefs are a little more sheltered by Taveuni Island but southeasterly winds still affect these offshore snorkel sites.

Where and who to go with

Accommodation on Taveuni may be able to arrange day trips to Waitabu Marine Reserve to snorkel. This is community led but can be exposed to the predominantly southeasterly winds.

The Qamea Homestay is a lovely village option but you need to take your own drinking water, meet the chief, and maybe stay a few days to get the best weather.

Otherwise, contact these operators to access nearby offshore sites when the conditions are good.

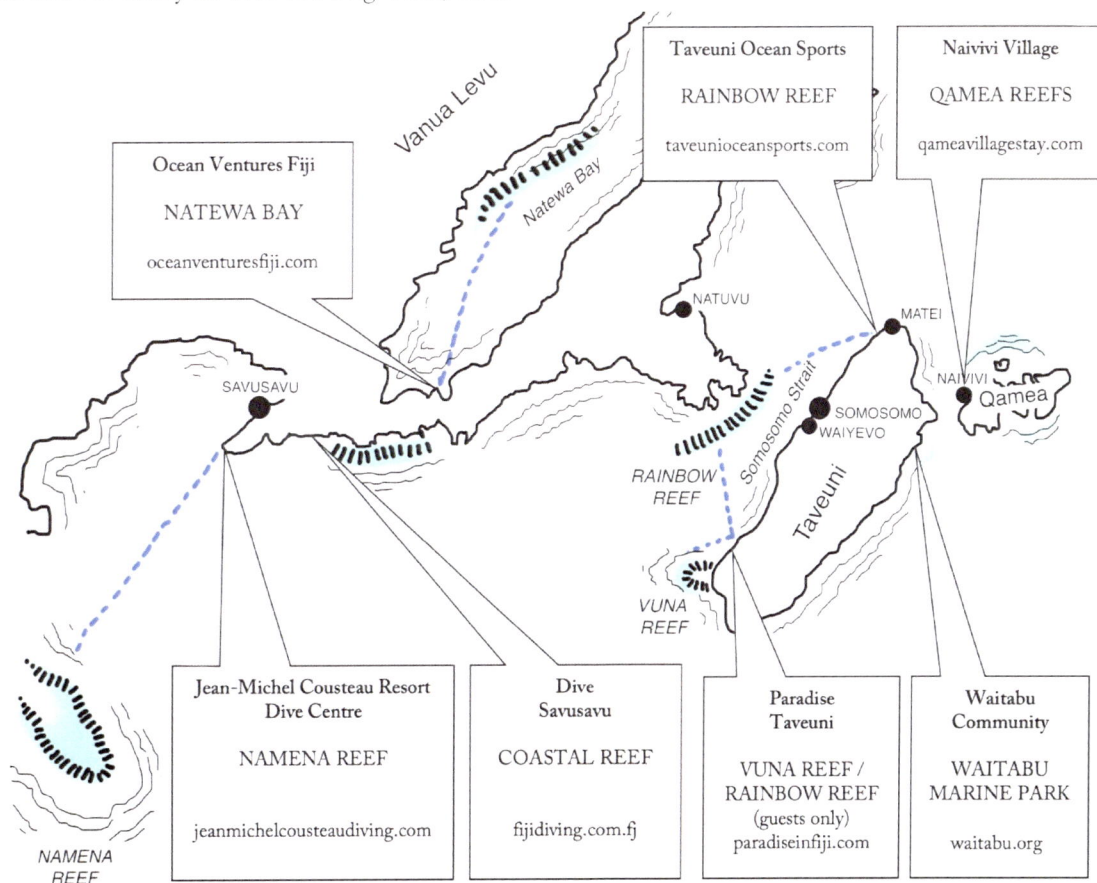

Ocean Ventures Fiji
NATEWA BAY
oceanventuresfiji.com

Taveuni Ocean Sports
RAINBOW REEF
taveunioceansports.com

Naivivi Village
QAMEA REEFS
qameavillagestay.com

Jean-Michel Cousteau Resort Dive Centre
NAMENA REEF
jeanmichelcousteaudiving.com

Dive Savusavu
COASTAL REEF
fijidiving.com.fj

Paradise Taveuni
VUNA REEF / RAINBOW REEF
(guests only)
paradiseinfiji.com

Waitabu Community
WAITABU MARINE PARK
waitabu.org

THIRTY more animals to look out for

In addition to the 38 species mentioned earlier in the book, here are another 30 to keep an eye out for. Almost all of the species mentioned could be seen at any of the snorkelling sites. Naturally this only a small taste of the diversity of what lives on Fiji's coral reefs but it will give you an introduction to the incredible diversity you could see in a short space of time. These species are named on p36.

1

2

3

4

14

15

16

17

18

19

20

21

22

23

24

25

27

26

28

29

30

List of animals mentioned in this book

SPECIES

P9 Spot-fin Lionfish
Leopard Blenny
Sailors Eyeball

P10 Small-scale Scorpionfish
Varicose Phyllidia
Dwarf Hawkfish.

P14 Stars and Stripes Pufferfish
Ringed Sap-sucking Slug
Banded Snake-eel
Tiger Cowry
Fiji Anemonefish
Brittlestar
Blue Sea Star Shrimp
Peppered Moray
Picasso Leatherjacket
Green Mantis Shrimp
Gymnodoris Sea Slug.

P18 Flabellina sea slug
Blue-spotted Trevally
Green Turtle
White-tipped Reef Shark

P20 Rockmover Wrasse
Purple Staghorn Coral
Jewelled Blenny
Minor Giant Clam.

P22 Crown-of-Thorns Seastar
Blue-spotted Hermit Crab

Reeftop Pipefish
Banded Sea Krait
Geography Cone.

P24 Halloween Hermit Crab
Day Octopus
Ringeye Hawkfish
Ocellated Dragonet
Giant Moray
Common Lionfish.

P33 Christmas Tree Worms

P37 Scissortail Sergeant

30 more animals to look out for

1. Black-tipped Reef Shark
2. Spinner Dolphin
3. Blue-spotted Fantail Ray
4. Hawksbill Turtle
5. White-spotted Hermit Crab
6. Banded Coral Shrimp
7. Coral Hermit Crab
8. Loch's Chromodoris
9. Featherstar / Crinoid (these come in many colours)
10. Leopard Sea Cucumber
11. Upside-down Jellyfish
12. Fissued Phylidiella
13. Graeff's Sea Cucumber
14. Yellow Boxfish
15. Fiji Fang Blenny
16. Lizardfish
17. Red-spotted Blenny
18. Honeycomb Rock Cod
19. Snowflake Moray
20. Mirror Basslet
21. Triangular Butterflyfish
22. South Seas Devil
23. Headband Dascyllus
24. Orange-finned Anemonefish
25. Six-barred Wrasse
26. Convict Tang
27. Titan Triggerfish
28. Spothead Grubfish
29. Harlequin Leatherjacket
30. Many-spotted Sweetlips

Additional photo credits, iStock © #20 Nigel Marsh, #21, #22 Francesco Ricciardi.

Image. Sunset over Savusavu Bay

Wind, tides and currents

WIND in this region is predominantly from the southeast. Snorkelling becomes difficult when the wind is above about 20kph and boat trips can be cancelled.

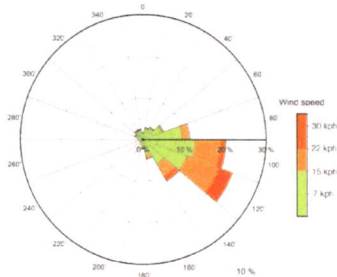

The wind rose shows how conditions above about 20 kph can be expected for 25-30% of the time. During these times it's best to be snorkelling on the leeward side of the islands, where the weather is calmest.

Figure adapted from Waves and Coasts in the Pacific (WACOP), SPC-Geoscience

Offshore wind (ideal)

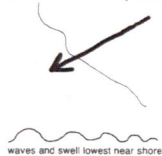

waves and swell lowest near shore

Onshore wind (poor)

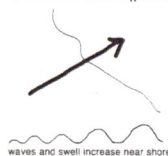

waves and swell increase near shore

⚠ **TIDES & CURRENTS** are vital considerations. In some cases there simply isn't enough water to cross reefs at low tide. In other cases, low tide is the only time that it is safe to snorkel. The current may change direction between incoming and outgoing tides, plus seawater draining off the top of reefs on falling tides, can create strong outgoing currents.

CYCLONES occur mostly between November and April, though occasionally, they have formed in October and May and rarely in September and June.

Image. Christmas Tree Worms

37

RAIN doesn't affect snorkelling but water quality can be tainted after heavy rain, as waste water reaches the sea from storm water drains. Generally speaking, it's best to avoid swimming near built-up areas after heavy rain storms.

Other advice

Dangerous Wildlife

SHARKS are common but incidents mostly involve spearfishers carrying bait. Nonetheless, it is best not to swim in poor visibility or at dawn or dusk. If you see a shark, face towards it and if it's curious, it may swim towards you. Stay calm and still and enjoy the spectacle.

SEA SNAKES are completely nonchalant and will not harm you if you leave them alone.

⚠ DO NOT TOUCH ANYTHING.

There is one animal that can kill you outright. Some Cone Shells are deadly. There is no cure for their lethal venom. Other animals such as lionfish and stonefish have very strong and painful toxin.

Behave nicely around animals

You are going to get your best encounters with wildlife if you go slow and allow animals to come to you. Don't be tempted to try to photograph everything. Your best photos will be the ones that are taken without forcing an outcome.

Once you're relaxed in the water you'll find animals are more curious – that is why it's good to practice the swimming techniques referred to earlier. If you see something of interest, take your time to get a sense of what the animal is doing. Not only will you see intriguing behaviour but it will allow time for wildlife to get comfortable in your presence.

Image. A patch of cabbage coral at SigaSiga Sands.

Underwater cameras

The standard for serious amateurs is the Olympus TG7 (below, left). A camera and housing will set you back about $1,000. A GoPro or equivalent is a good option for beginners. These days you can also buy universal housing for smart phones (below, right). The units start at about $250.

Want professional advice?

For up-to-date advice contact Underwater Australasia. Follow the link in this QR Code …

Be sure to mention this book and Wildiaries.

More reading

Weather
Fiji Met Office https://www.met.gov.fj/index.php?page=marine
Windy.app (Google Play / Appled Store)

Tides
Seatemperatu.re https://www.seatemperatu.re/oceania/fiji/savusavu/tides.html

Wildlife
Fiji Islands World of Water Wildlife Guide, Neville Coleman
iNaturalist   https://inaturalist.ala.org.au/users/sign_in

About Simon Mustoe

Simon Mustoe is a conservationist, expeditioner, artist and author of *Wildlife in the Balance: Why Animals are Humanity's Best Hope.* Telling the story about our relationship with and dependence on wildlife is Simon's passion.

Simon has worked all over the world as an ecologist, expeditioner and conservationist. He's tumbled in boats amid frigid North Atlantic storms, trekked solo into Madagascar's remote dry forests, discovered unknown species of seabird in Australia's tropical ocean territories and recorded previously unseen whales in West Papua.

He co-produced Australia's National Landscapes Nature Series, blogs to a quarter of a million people. And continues to play an active role as adviser to important ecosystem restoration initiatives.

simonmustoe.blog

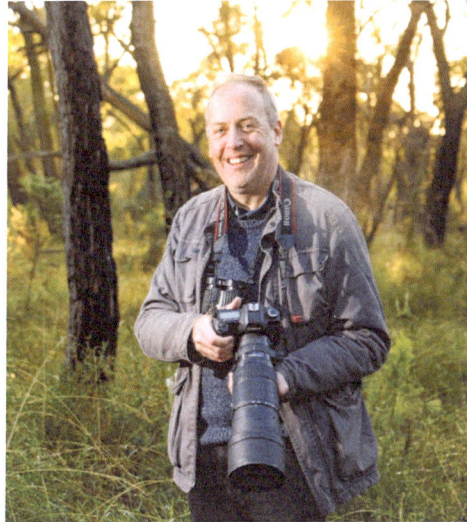

Read *Wildlife in the Balanc*

"Important beyond compare, utterly engrossing, at once chilling and heartening."
Dame Joanna Lumley

"A captivating literary masterpiece"
Salon Privé Magazine

Drawing upon extensive research and his own personal experience as a conservationist, Mustoe takes the reader on a fascinating journey through some of the planet's most spectacular wildlife events, to learn how the world works, the origin of life and our place in nature.

Image: Scissortail Sergeants at Split Rock

www.ingramcontent.com/pod-product-compliance
Lightning Source LLC
Chambersburg PA
CBRC101843030426
42334CB00009BA/122